Disclaimers

I0437738

Cal/OSHA Consultation Service, Research and Education Unit,
Division of Occupational Safety and Health, California Department of Industrial Relations.

Ergonomic Guidelines for Manual Material Handling was prepared for publication by the Cal/OSHA Consultation Service, Research and Education Unit, Division of Occupational Safety and Health, California Department of Industrial Relations.

It was distributed under the provisions of the Library Distribution Act and *Government Code* Section 11096.

Published 2007 by the California Department of Industrial Relations

Foreword

Manual material handling (MMH) work contributes to a large percentage of the over half a million cases of musculoskeletal disorders reported annually in the United States. Musculoskeletal disorders often involve strains and sprains to the lower back, shoulders, and upper limbs. They can result in protracted pain, disability, medical treatment, and financial stress for those afflicted with them, and employers often find themselves paying the bill, either directly or through workers' compensation insurance, at the same time they must cope with the loss of the full capacity of their workers.

Scientific evidence shows that effective ergonomic interventions can lower the physical demands of MMH work tasks, thereby lowering the incidence and severity of the musculoskeletal injuries they can cause. Their potential for reducing injury-related costs alone make ergonomic interventions a useful tool for improving a company's productivity, product quality, and overall business competitiveness. But very often productivity gets an additional and solid shot in the arm when managers and workers take a fresh look at how best to use energy, equipment, and exertion to get the job done in the most efficient, effective, and effortless way possible. Planning that applies these principles can result in big wins for all concerned.

This booklet will help you to recognize high-risk MMH work tasks and choose effective options for reducing their physical demands.

Illustrated inside you will find approaches like:

- Eliminating lifting from the floor and using simple transport devices like carts or dollies
- Using lift-assist devices like scissors lift tables or load levelers
- Using more sophisticated equipment like powered stackers, hoists, cranes, or vacuum assist devices
- Guiding your choice of equipment by analyzing and redesigning work stations and workflow

NIOSH and Cal/OSHA are dedicated to finding the bottom line in state-of the-art-research and turning the results into practical guidance for improving the safety and health of all workers. We hope you find the MMH booklet a useful and effective example of our efforts.

John Howard, M.D.
Director, NIOSH

Len Welsh, M.S., J.D.
Acting Chief, Cal/OSHA

Partners

The following organizations are responsible for the development and co-publishing of this booklet. To obtain copies of this booklet, contact any of the partners listed below.

Cal/OSHA Consultation Service
Research and Education Unit
2211 Park Towne Circle, #4
Sacramento, CA 95825
Tel: (916) 574-2528
http://www.dir.ca.gov/dosh/reu
http://www.dir.ca.gov/dosh/puborder.asp

CNA Insurance Companies
333 S. Wabash Ave.
Chicago, IL 60604
Tel: (866) 262-0504
http://www.cna.com

Ergonomic Assist Systems and Equipment (EASE)
a Product Council of Material Handling Industry of America (MHIA)
8720 Red Oak Blvd., Suite 201
Charlotte, NC 28217-3992
Tel: (704) 676-1190
http://www.mhia.org/EASE

National Institute for Occupational Safety and Health (NIOSH)
Centers for Disease Control and Prevention
4676 Columbia Parkway
Cincinnati, OH 45226-1998
Tel: 1-800-35-NIOSH (1-800-356-4674)
http://www.cdc.gov/niosh

Contents

About This Booklet

This booklet is written for managers and supervisors in industries that involve the manual handling of containers. It offers suggestions to improve the handling of rectangular, square, and cylindrical containers, sacks, and bags.

"Improving Manual Material Handling in Your Workplace" lists the benefits of improving your work tasks. It also contains information on risk factors, types of ergonomic improvements, and effective training and sets out a four-step proactive action plan. The plan helps you identify problems, set priorities, make changes, and follow up.

Sections 1 and 2 of "Improvement Options" provide ways to improve lifting, lowering, filling, emptying, or carrying tasks by changing work practices and/or the use of equipment. Guidelines for safer work practices are also included.

Section 3 of "Improvement Options" provides ideas for using equipment instead of manually handling individual containers. Guidelines for safer equipment use are also included.

For more help the **"Resources"** section contains additional information on administrative improvements, work assessment tools and comprehensive analysis methods. This section also includes an improvement evaluation tool and a list of professional and trade organizations related to material handling.

Improving Manual Material Handling in Your Workplace

What Manual Material Handling Is

According to the U.S. Department of Labor, *handling* is defined as:

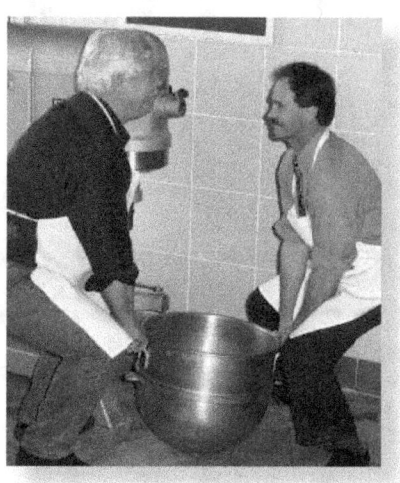

Seizing, holding, grasping, turning, or otherwise working with the hand or hands. Fingers are involved only to the extent that they are an extension of the hand, such as to turn a switch or to shift automobile gears.

*In this publication, **handling** means that the worker's hands move individual containers manually by lifting, lowering, filling, emptying, or carrying them.*

Why Improve Your Workplace

Manual handling of containers may expose workers to physical conditions (e.g., force, awkward postures, and repetitive motions) that can lead to injuries, wasted energy, and wasted time. To avoid these problems, your organization can directly benefit from ***improving the fit*** between the demands of work tasks and the capabilities of your workers. Remember that workers' abilities to perform work tasks may vary because of differences in age, physical condition, strength, gender, stature, and other factors. In short, changing your workplace by ***improving the fit*** can benefit your workplace by:

- Reducing or preventing injuries

- Reducing workers' efforts by decreasing forces in lifting, handling, pushing, and pulling materials

- Reducing risk factors for musculoskeletal disorders (e.g., awkward postures from reaching into containers)

- Increasing productivity, product and service quality, and worker morale

- Lowering costs by reducing or eliminating production bottlenecks, error rates or rejects, use of medical services because of musculoskeletal disorders, workers' compensation claims, excessive worker turnover, absenteeism, and retraining

What to Look for

Manual material handling tasks may expose workers to physical risk factors. If these tasks are performed repeatedly or over long periods of time, they can lead to fatigue and injury. The main risk factors, or *conditions,* associated with the development of injuries in manual material handling tasks include:

- Awkward postures (e.g., bending, twisting)
- Repetitive motions (e.g., frequent reaching, lifting, carrying)
- Forceful exertions (e.g., carrying or lifting heavy loads)
- Pressure points (e.g., grasping [or contact from] loads, leaning against parts or surfaces that are hard or have sharp edges)
- Static postures (e.g., maintaining fixed positions for a long time)

Repeated or continual exposure to one or more of these factors initially may lead to fatigue and discomfort. Over time, injury to the back, shoulders, hands, wrists, or other parts of the body may occur. Injuries may include damage to muscles, tendons, ligaments, nerves, and blood vessels. Injuries of this type are known as musculoskeletal disorders, or **MSDs.**

In addition, poor environmental conditions, such as extreme heat, cold, noise, and poor lighting, may increase workers' chances of developing other types of problems.

Types of Ergonomic Improvements

In general, ergonomic improvements are changes made to *improve the fit* between the demands of work tasks and the capabilities of your workers. There are usually many options for improving a particular manual handling task. It is up to you to make informed choices about which improvements will work best for particular tasks.

There are two types of ergonomic improvements:

1. Engineering improvements
2. Administrative improvements

1. Engineering Improvements

These include rearranging, modifying, redesigning, providing or replacing tools, equipment, workstations, packaging, parts, processes, products, or materials (see "Improvement Options").

2. Administrative Improvements

Observe how different workers perform the same tasks to get ideas for improving work practices or organizing the work. Then consider the following improvements:

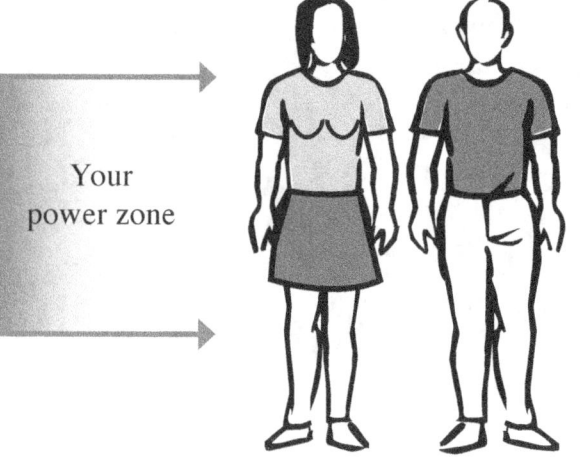

Your power zone

- Alternate heavy tasks with light tasks.
- Provide variety in jobs to eliminate or reduce repetition (i.e., overuse of the same muscle groups).
- Adjust work schedules, work pace, or work practices.
- Provide recovery time (e.g., short rest breaks).
- Modify work practices so that workers perform work within their power zone (i.e., above the knees, below the shoulders, and close to the body).
- Rotate workers through jobs that use different muscles, body parts, or postures.

Administrative improvements, such as job rotation, can help reduce workers' exposures to risk factors by limiting the amount of time workers spend on "problem jobs." However, these measures may still expose workers to risk factors that can lead to injuries. For these reasons, the most effective way to eliminate "problem jobs" is to change them. This can be done by putting into place the appropriate engineering improvements and modifying work practices accordingly.

Training

Training alone is not an ergonomic improvement. Instead, it should be used together with any workplace changes made. Workers need training and hands-on practice with new tools, equipment, or work practices to make sure they have the skills necessary to work safely. Training is most effective when it is interactive and fully involves workers. Below are some suggestions for training based on adult learning principles:

- Provide hands-on practice when new tools, equipment, or procedures are introduced to the workforce.
- Use several types of visual aids (e.g., pictures, charts, videos) of actual tasks in your workplace.
- Hold small-group discussions and problem-solving sessions.
- Give workers ample opportunity for questions.

A Proactive Action Plan

Manual material handling jobs require movement and physical activity. But how do you find out:

- Why workplace problems are occurring?
- Which work tasks may be causing injuries or production bottlenecks or decreasing product and service quality?
- What to do about problems once you find them?
- How to reduce your workers' compensation costs?

One way to answer these questions is to be **proactive** in your problem solving. Being **proactive** simply means finding the problems first by looking thoroughly around the workplace rather than waiting for problems to occur. Then improve the fit between the work and the worker by putting the appropriate changes into place.

The process includes involving workers, observing jobs, making decisions on effective options, and then taking action. It is important to involve workers, managers, and supervisors throughout the process.

There are four steps to a proactive action plan:

1. Look for clues.
2. Prioritize jobs for improvements.
3. Make improvements.
4. Follow up.

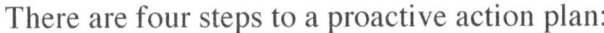

Step 1: Look for Clues

a. *Review written records* (e.g., OSHA Log 300, past worker reports or complaints, and workers' compensation reports). Your workers' compensation insurance carrier may offer risk-management services that can provide workplace assessment surveys.

b. *Observe work activities.* Talk to workers, supervisors, and managers about where problems exist. Look for warning signs, such as:

- Risk factors in work tasks (e.g., awkward postures, repetitive motions, forceful exertions, pressure points, staying in the same position for a long time)

- Worker fatigue, discomfort, or reports of related problems

- Workers exhibiting "pain behaviors" (e.g., not moving body parts, self-restricting their movements, or massaging hands, arms, legs, necks, or backs)

- Workers modifying tools, equipment, or workstations on their own

- Increase in absenteeism, worker turnover rates, or customer complaints

- Decrease in product or service quality or employee morale

- Increase in error rates, rejects, or wasted materials

- Production bottlenecks

- Malfunctioning equipment

- Missed deadlines

- Unnecessary handling and duplication of material and product movement

Make sure to talk to your workers about their ideas for altering work processes, operations, tools, or equipment. Ask them how they would make their jobs less physically demanding and more efficient.

c. *Use assessment tools* - To determine where problems may arise in work tasks, you may want to use some of the following simple "tools" (see Appendix B):

- NIOSH Manual Material Handling Checklist

- NIOSH Hazard Evaluation Checklist for Lifting, Pushing, or Pulling

- The Awareness Worksheet: Looking for Clues

- Ergonomics Checklist - Material Handling

If the problems are complex, more sophisticated methods may be needed for addressing your workplace MSDs. More detailed assessment tools for specific problems include the following (see Appendix C):

- NIOSH Lifting Equation

- American Conference of Governmental Industrial Hygienists (ACGIH) Threshold Limit Values (TLVs) for Manual Lifting

- University of Michigan 3D Static Strength Prediction Program

- Ohio State University Lumbar Motion Monitor

- Snook's Psychophysical Tables

Step 2: Prioritize Jobs for Improvements

After detecting the problems, decide which tasks to improve and then set priorities. Consider:

- The frequency and severity of the risk factors you have identified that may lead to injuries
- The frequency and severity of complaints, symptoms, and/or injuries
- Technical and financial resources at your disposal
- Ideas of workers for making improvements
- Difficulty in implementing various improvements
- Timeframe for making improvements

Step 3: Make Improvements

The goal of making changes is to ***improve the fit*** between the demands of work tasks and the capabilities of your workers. Combine operations and processes whenever possible to reduce or eliminate unnecessary manual handling of materials and products. *Depending on the characteristics of the work and the workers, there may be some changes that will improve a particular task.*

For suggestions on how to improve your work tasks, see "Improvement Options."

Appendix D contains a tool to help evaluate the improvements you are considering.

If you need additional help with improvements, consider the following:

- **Talk to various employees**. Brainstorming with engineers, maintenance personnel, managers, and production workers is a great way to generate ideas.
- **Contact others in your industry**. They may have solutions that could also apply to your problem, saving you time, money, and effort.
- **Look through equipment catalogs**. Focus on equipment dealing with the types of problems you are trying to solve.
- **Talk to equipment vendors**. They may be able to share ideas from operations similar to yours.
- **Consult with an expert in ergonomics**. An expert can provide insights into available improvements, the cost, and the potential value.
- **Call Cal/OSHA Consultation Service** (only for businesses located in California). It provides free on-site consultation and advice on occupational safety and health.
- **Search the Internet** (e.g., Material Handling Industry of America, www.mhia.org, Material Handling Equipment Distributors Association, www.mheda.org). See **Appendix E** for a list of resources on handling materials.

Step 4: Follow Up

It is important to follow up in order to evaluate if your improvements have worked. After a reasonable adjustment period, set a date to follow up on the changes made. Make sure to evaluate each improvement separately for effectiveness. The following questions may be helpful:

Has each improvement:

- Reduced or eliminated fatigue, discomfort, symptoms, and/or injuries?
- Been accepted by workers?
- Reduced or eliminated most or all of the risk factors?
- Caused any new risk factors, hazards, or other problems?
- Caused a decrease in productivity and efficiency?
- Caused a decrease in product and service quality?
- Been supported with the training needed to make it effective?

If you determine that your improvements have not worked, *modify them or try something different until the risk factors have been reduced or eliminated.*

Improvement Options

Section 1 — Easier Ways to Manually Lift, Lower, Fill, or Empty Containers

Pages 17–28

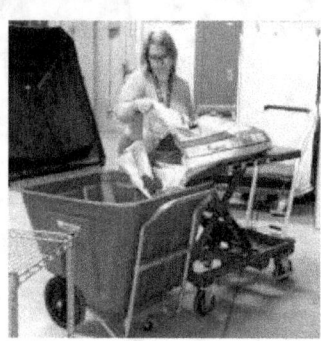

Consider the following options that will:

- Reduce reaching and bending.
- Reduce the stress on your back and shoulders.
- Reduce the effort and force needed to perform work tasks.

Section 2 — Easier Ways to Manually Carry Containers

Pages 29–34

Consider the following options that will:

- Improve your grip.
- Reduce stress on your back and shoulders.
- Reduce contact pressure on your shoulders and hands.
- Reduce the effort and force needed to perform work tasks.

Section 3 — Alternatives to Manual Handling of Individual Containers

Pages 35–48

- Change the container.
- Use a tool.
- Use non-powered equipment.
- Use powered equipment.

Easier Ways to Manually Lift, Lower, Fill, or Empty Containers

Consider the following options that will:

- Reduce reaching and bending.
- Reduce the stress on your back and shoulders.
- Reduce the effort and force needed to perform work tasks.

NIOSH Lifting Equation

The Revised National Institute of Occupational Safety and Health (NIOSH) Lifting Equation (1994) provides guidelines for evaluating two-handed manual lifting tasks. It defines a Recommended Weight Limit (RWL) as the weight of the load that nearly all healthy workers can lift over a substantial period of time (e.g., eight hours) without an increased risk of developing lower back pain. The maximum weight to be lifted with two hands, **under ideal conditions**, is 51 pounds. The RWL is based on six variables that reduce the maximum weight to be lifted to less than 51 pounds.

Consult the Revised NIOSH Lifting Equation (1994) for information to help assess complex lifting tasks (see Appendix C).

Note: **The lifting guidelines suggested by the Revised NIOSH Lifting Equation are not Cal/OSHA regulatory requirements and are not part of Title 8 of the *California Code of Regulations*.**

Management Guidelines for Safer Lifting

- Plan the workflow to eliminate unnecessary lifts.
- Organize the work so that the physical demands and work pace increase gradually.
- Minimize the distances loads are lifted and lowered.
- Position pallet loads of materials at a height that allows workers to lift and lower within their power zone.
- Avoid manually lifting or lowering loads to or from the floor.
  - Store materials and/or products off the floor.
  - Arrange materials to arrive on pallets, and keep materials on pallets during storage. Use a forklift to lift or lower the entire pallet of material, rather than lifting or lowering the material individually.
  - Arrange to have material off-loaded directly onto storage shelves. Store only lightweight or infrequently lifted items on the floor.
  - Use mechanical devices (e.g., lifts, hoists) whenever possible.
  - Avoid designing jobs that require workers to lift or lower materials to or from floor level.
- For loads that are unstable and/or heavy:
  - Tag the load to alert workers.
  - Test the load for stability and weight before carrying the load.
  - Use mechanical devices or equipment to lift the load.
  - Reduce the weight of the load by:
    - > Putting fewer items in the container.
    - > Using a smaller and/or lighter-weight container.
  - Repack containers so contents will not shift and the weight is balanced.
  - Use team lifting as a temporary measure for heavy or bulky objects.
- Reduce the frequency of lifting and the amount of time employees perform lifting tasks by:
  - Rotating workers in lifting tasks with other workers in non-lifting tasks.
  - Having workers alternate lifting tasks with non-lifting tasks.
- Clear spaces to improve access to materials or products being handled. Easy access allows workers to get closer and reduces reaching, bending, and twisting.

Employee Guidelines for Safer Lifting

- **The use of stretching is appropriate as part of a comprehensive ergonomic program. Stretching must not be used in place of engineering and/or administrative improvements**.

- Check for tags on loads.

- Before lifting, always test the load for stability and weight.

- For loads that are unstable and/or heavy, follow management guidelines for:
  - Equipment use
  - Reducing the weight of the load
  - Repacking containers to increase stability

- Plan the lift:
  - Wear appropriate shoes to avoid slips, trips, or falls.
  - If you wear gloves, choose the size that fits properly. Depending on the material the gloves are made of and the number of pairs worn at once, more force may be needed to grasp and hold objects. For example, wearing a single pair of heat-resistant gloves can reduce your grip strength up to 40 percent. Wearing two or more pairs of gloves at once can reduce your grip strength up to 60 percent.
  - Lift only as much as you can safely handle by yourself.
  - Keep the lifts in your power zone (i.e., above the knees, below the shoulders, and close to the body), if possible.
  - Use extra caution when lifting loads that may be unstable.

- When lifting:
  - Get a secure grip.
  - Use both hands whenever possible.
  - Avoid jerking by using smooth, even motions.
  - Keep the load as close to the body as possible.
  - To the extent feasible use your legs to push up and lift the load, not the upper body or back.
  - Do not twist your body. Step to one side or the other to turn.
  - Alternate heavy lifting or forceful exertion tasks with less physically demanding tasks.
  - Take rest breaks.

 Avoid lifting from the floor whenever possible. If you must lift from the floor, do not bend at the waist. The techniques shown below help the worker to keep the spine in a safer position while lifting from the floor.

Caution: This technique may be effective only if loads are small, light weight, and can easily fit between the knees.

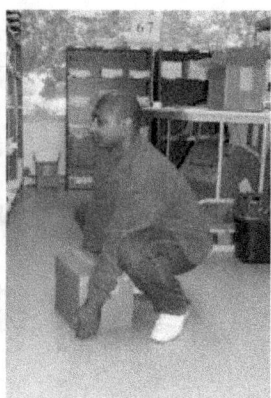 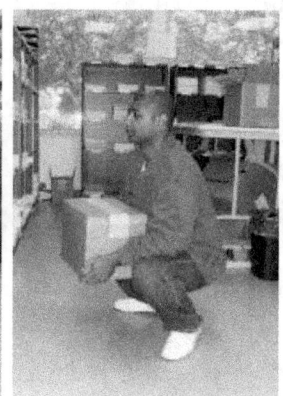  

Keep the load close to your body and lift by pushing up with your legs.

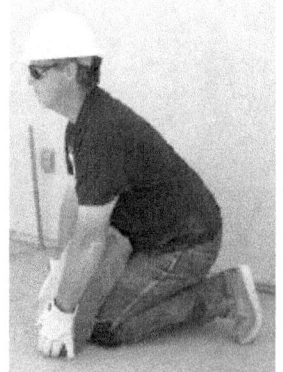 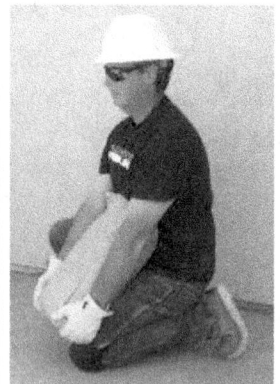 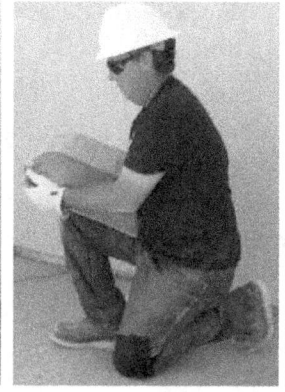 

Lean the sack onto your kneeling leg.

Slide the sack up onto your kneeling leg.

Slide the sack onto the other leg while keeping the sack close to your body.

As you stand up, keep the sack close to your body.

Use team lifting as a temporary measure until a more permanent improvement can be found. If possible, try to find a co-worker of similar height to help with the lift.

Caution:
Team lifting can increase the risk of a slip, trip, or fall accident.

Team lifting can reduce the load in half.
Discuss your lifting plan so you
don't make surprise movements.

Use a scissors lift, load lifter, or pneumatic lifter to raise or lower the load so that it is level with the work surface. Then slide the load instead of lifting.

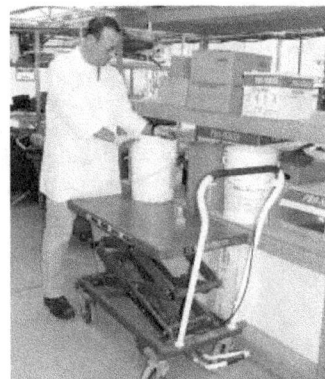 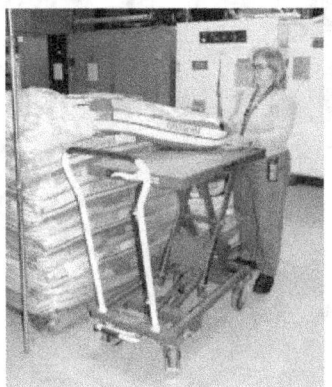  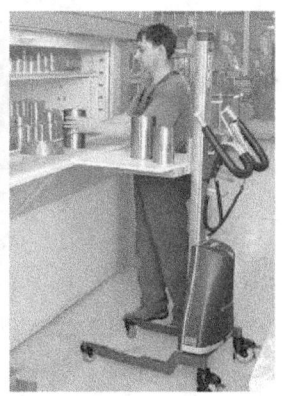

Scissors lifts

Pneumatic lifter
(accordion skirting)

Adjust the load
lifter to shelf
level and remove
containers by
sliding them out.

 Use a turntable. Rotate the turntable to bring the container closer. Always work from the side closest to the load.

Turntable on a load leveler

A fixed-height turntable for pallets with short low stacks.

Caution: To promote stability when loading and unloading, rotate the turntable occasionally to avoid the buildup of the load on one side.

Table with a turntable inset

Turntable on a cart

 Use a tool.

This pot lifter reduces bending and reaching when handling pots or other cylindrical containers (see Appendix E, page 64, University of California Agricultural Ergonomics Research Center, UC Davis).

Raise the worker so that the container is grasped 30"– 40" from the surface the worker is standing on.

Use a step stool.

Use portable steps.

Use catwalks or platforms.

Use a portable work platform and adjust it to the height of the worker.

> **!** *Caution:* When using portable steps, stools, catwalks, or other work platforms, follow all manufacturers' recommendations for proper use. Use only equipment appropriate to the weight, size, and shape of the load being handled.

 Work within your power zone. Raise or lower the work surface.

Stack pallets to create a higher work surface.

Use electric or pneumatic scissors lift (accordion skirting).

Use powered stackers.

Provide variable-height work surfaces.

 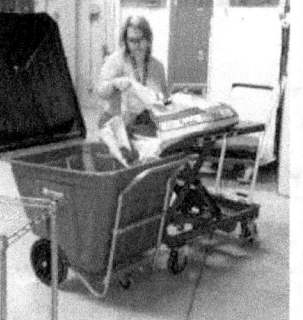

Use mobile scissors lifts.

Use stationary scissors lift.

 Store heavier or bulkier containers so that they can be handled within your power zone where you have the greatest strength and most comfort.

 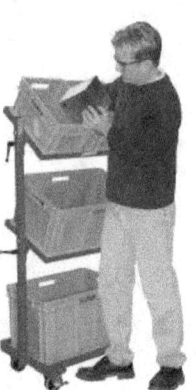

Work within your power zone. Tilt the container to improve handling of materials.

 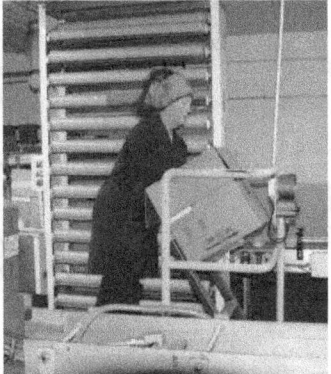 

Use fixed or adjustable tilt stands for smaller containers.

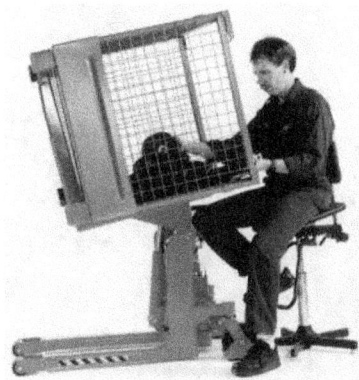

Powered tilters provide better access to large containers.

Use angled shelving to improve access to containers.

Hold the container close to the body when lifting and lowering.

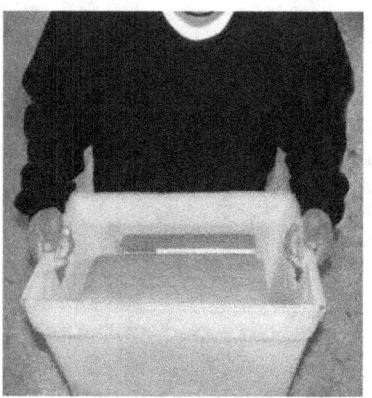

For easier access, remove or lower the sides of the receptacle.

Add extra handles for better grip and control.

Support the container on or against a fixed object, rack, or stand while pouring the contents.

Use a removable plate or a work surface to support the container while pouring the contents into the receptacle.

Use a screen over the opening to support the sack. Pour the contents through the screen.

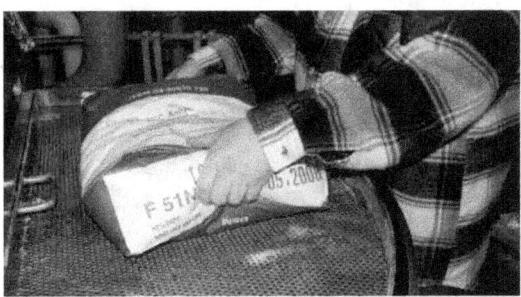

 Use a cutout work surface so that you can get closer to the container.

 Use a pail tipper.

Manual pail tippers are available for 1-, 2-, and 5-gallon containers.

Easier Ways to Manually Carry Containers

Consider the following options that will:

- Improve your grip.
- Reduce stress on your back and shoulders.
- Reduce contact pressure on your shoulders and hands.
- Reduce the effort and force needed to perform work tasks.

- Plan the workflow to eliminate unnecessary carrying.

- Slide, push, or roll instead of carrying, when appropriate.

- Organize the work so that the physical demands and work pace increase gradually.

- Reduce the distances that loads are moved to a minimum. If long trips are required, use equipment.

- For loads that are unstable and/or heavy:

  - Tag the load to alert workers.
  - Test the load for stability and weight before carrying the load.
  - Use mechanical devices or equipment to carry or move the load.
  - Reduce the weight of the load by:

    > Putting fewer things in the container.
    > Using smaller and/or lighter weight containers.
    > Dividing the load between two containers and carrying one in each hand.

  - Repack the containers so contents will not shift and the weight is balanced.
  - Use team carrying as a temporary measure for heavy or bulky objects.

- Reduce the frequency and amount of time workers carry materials by:

  - Rotating workers in carrying tasks with other workers in non-carrying tasks.
  - Having workers alternate carrying tasks with non-carrying tasks.

- **The use of stretching is appropriate as part of a comprehensive ergonomic program. Stretching must not be used in place of engineering and/or administrative improvements.**

- Check for tags on loads.

- Before carrying, always test the load for stability and weight.

- For long trips or loads that are unstable and/or heavy, follow management guidelines for:
  - Equipment use.
  - Reducing the weight of the load.
  - Repacking containers to increase stability.

- Plan before carrying:
  - Wear appropriate shoes to avoid slips, trips or falls.
  - If you wear gloves choose the size that fits properly. Depending on the material the gloves are made of and the number of pairs worn at once, more force may be needed to grasp and hold objects. For example, wearing a single pair of heat resistant gloves can reduce your grip strength up to 40 percent. Wearing two or more pairs of gloves at once can reduce your grip strength up to 60 percent.
  - Avoid carrying large or bulky loads that limit or obstruct your vision.
  - Slide, push, or roll instead of carrying when appropriate.
  - When there is a choice, push instead of pull.
  - Carry only as much as you can safely handle by yourself.
  - Try to avoid slopes, stairs, or other obstacles that make carrying materials more difficult.
  - Beware of and try to avoid slippery floors (e.g., liquids, ice, oil, and fine powders).
  - Use extra caution when moving loads that may be unstable.

- When carrying:
  - Keep loads close to your body.
  - Make sure you have a clear view of the path.
  - When carrying containers with one hand, alternate hands.
  - Whenever appropriate, use two hands to carry containers.
  - Alternate heavy or forceful exertion tasks with less physically demanding tasks.
  - Take rest breaks.

 Redesign the container so it has handles, grips, or handholds.

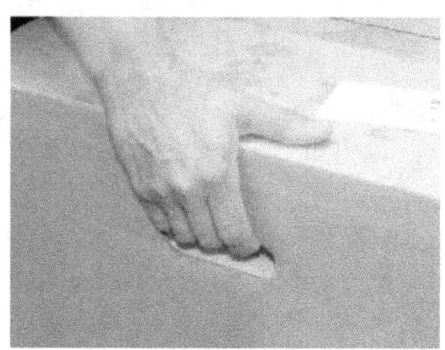

 Hold the container close to the body.

 Don't carry more than you can handle. To reduce the weight of the load, use a smaller container.

Wear proper size gloves that fit. Gloves with rubber dots on the surface can increase grip stability on slippery surfaces.

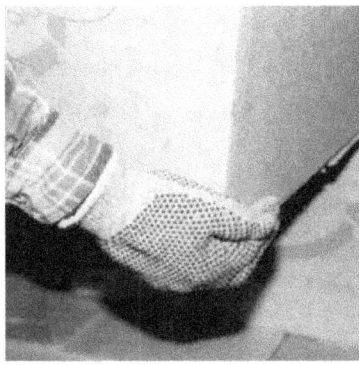 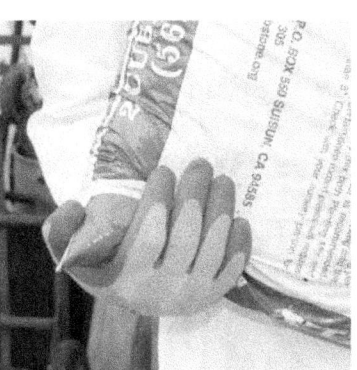

> *Caution:*
> Be aware that gloves can reduce your grip strength up to 60 percent depending on the material they are made of and how many pairs you wear at once.

Increase the size of the bucket or pail handle with padding or a clamp-on handle.

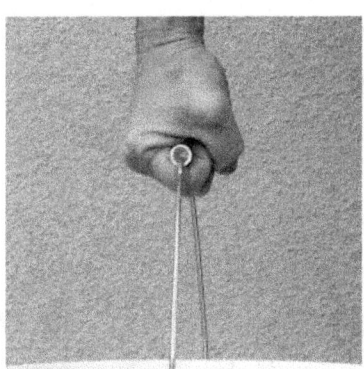 

Get co-worker assistance when necessary. Discuss your plan so you don't have surprise movements.

Pad the shoulder. Support the container on one shoulder and alternate between shoulders.

Use equipment to carry materials whenever possible. If you must manually carry materials on your shoulder, reduce the weight of the load and use a pad to provide a cushion.

Use a tool.

Pinch grips involve grasping items with the thumb and the tips of the other fingers. Power grips involve grasping items by wrapping all the fingers around an object. When grasping objects (e.g., handles) with a diameter of 1.25 – 2 inches and a straight wrist, power grips can provide up to 75% more strength compared with pinch grips.

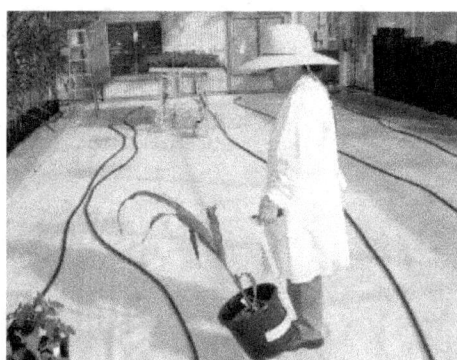

This pot lifter makes carrying pots and other cylindrical containers easier. It replaces a pinch grip with a power grip and a straight wrist. It also allows for an upright posture (see Appendix E, page 64, University of California Agricultural Ergonomics Research Center, UC Davis).

Alternatives to Manual Handling of Individual Containers

- Change the container.
- Use a tool.
- Use non-powered equipment.
- Use powered equipment.

Equipment

- Know your load and buy equipment of appropriate capacity. Remember, lighter-weight equipment is easier to move.

- Choose equipment appropriate for the material(s) being handled, the layout and design of your workplace, and the work tasks being performed (see Appendix B).

- Consider using powered equipment —rather than non-powered— when pushing and pulling forces are excessive (see Appendix C, Snook's Psychophysical Tables).

- If available, select equipment with vertical handles so workers' hands can be in their power zone.

- Choose wheeled equipment which minimizes start forces (inertia) and reduces rolling resistance. The amount of force required to move loads with wheeled equipment depends on a number of factors including the:
  - Weight and shape of the load
  - Type and condition of the floor surface (e.g., smoothness, density, and other factors)
  - Route taken (e.g., slopes, obstacles, and other factors)
  - Type of wheels (i.e., the materials they are made of)
  - Size of wheels (larger wheels a minimum of 6 inches in diameter move more easily over holes, bumps, and floor irregularities)
  - Maintenance of wheels; it is important to clean, lubricate, and/or replace wheels on a regular basis.

- Ground all electrically operated equipment

- Make sure equipment alarms and warning devices are audible and working properly.

- Inspect and maintain equipment according to manufacturers' recommendations.

- Follow all manufacturers' recommendations for proper equipment use.

Work Environment

- Clear the aisles and doorways for safe passage and maneuvering of equipment.

- Set barriers that prevent employees from coming close to or beneath supported or moving loads.

- In tight spaces, use equipment with four swivel casters or wheels. Loads are easier to turn and control.

Work Practices

- Train employees on proper equipment use and appropriate work practices.

- Push and pull equipment with the entire body instead of with just the arms and shoulders.

- When pushing or pulling use both hands when feasible.

- To move heavy loads over long distances, either reduce the load or use powered equipment.

- Inspect pallets before loading or moving them.

Change the container

Instead of lifting and pouring from the drum, insert a siphon or a pump.

 *Caution:* To prevent cross-contamination, chemical incompatibility, and flammability hazards, do not interchange pumps or siphons among different containers.

Increase the size of the container or the weight of the load so that it is too large to handle manually.

Use a tool

Use a hook for light-weight containers to reduce your reach.

Use non-powered equipment

Use a drum dolly.

The drum must be set down into this dolly.

This drum dolly lifts and transports drums.

Use a cart or platform truck.

A hand cart can have multiple shelves for moving a variety of containers at one time.

This six-wheel platform truck is easy to maneuver and will turn in its own length.

This three-wheel cart transports but does not lift drums.

Two-wheel carts work well for loads up to about 300 pounds.

Use a portable scissors lift.

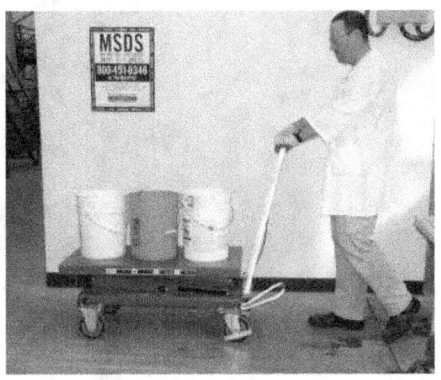

This scissors lift has a foot pump to raise or lower the platform so the containers can be slid on or off.

Use a hand truck.

This specialty hand truck with brakes will allow more control when heavy loads are on inclines.

Another type of hand truck converts to four wheels for moving unstable loads.

Hand trucks can be fitted with trays to carry bottles.

Two-wheel hand trucks work well for transporting bottles or cylinders over short distances.

Some hand trucks are specially designed for transporting cylinders.

This hand truck has an additional handle to provide better directional control.

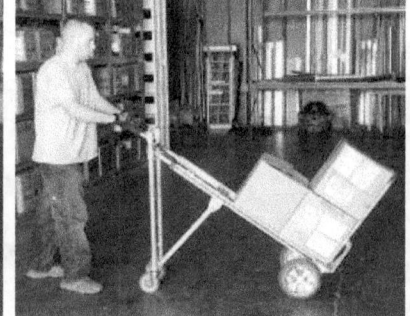

This hand truck fitted with retractable rear wheels converts into a flatbed cart.

Use a conveyor, slide, or chute.

Design a conveyor system that delivers the container directly into position for loading.

Use slides or chutes to do the work if containers are always moving in one direction.

Use spiral conveyors or chutes where space is limited.

Small containers and lightweight loads can be handled by gravity conveyors.

Gravity-activated conveyors work well for short, downhill runs.

A curved skate-wheel conveyor moves containers around corners. It is activated by gravity.

Skate-wheel conveyors can be easily set up wherever needed and work well for light loads.

Floor-mounted roller conveyors can handle heavier pallet loads.

An expandable skate-wheel conveyor is portable and excellent where work needs to have a flexible layout.

Use non-powered equipment

Non-powered hand pallet trucks are useful for moving loads over short distances when low forces are required. For moving heavy loads requiring high forces over long distances it is advantageous to use powered pallet trucks.

Use a hand pallet truck.

When using hand pallet trucks, be sure the floor is smooth and free of debris.

For unstable pallet loads, wrap straps around the load.

Use a portable hoist or crane.

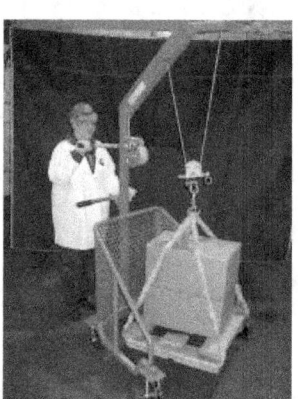

A portable hoist or "cherry picker" is manually operated. It is convenient for occasional spot-lifting of heavy loads.

Portable gantry cranes are adjustable in height. They can be fitted with manual, electric, or pneumatic hoists for moving heavy loads over short distances.

Use non-powered equipment

Use powered equipment

Use a stacker.

This stacker is well suited for moving loads up to 3,000 pounds for short distances.

This stacker is fitted with a special drum-handling attachment.

Stackers can be fitted with specially shaped forks to handle round or cylindrical containers.

Use a powered hand truck.

This is a powered two-wheel hand truck designed for climbing stairs.

Use an airball table.

An airball table makes it easier to slide containers, thereby reducing workers' efforts.

Use a forklift.

A forklift moves pallets long distances.

Special attachments are available for removing cartons layer by layer.

Use a crane.

A portable gantry crane fitted with an electric hoist

A workstation crane fitted with a balancer and a vacuum lifter for handling large or heavy containers

A jib crane fitted with an electric hoist and a lifting tong

Use a pallet truck.

Use a lifter.

A manually propelled load lifter carries containers. The power lift raises and lowers containers to the appropriate work height.

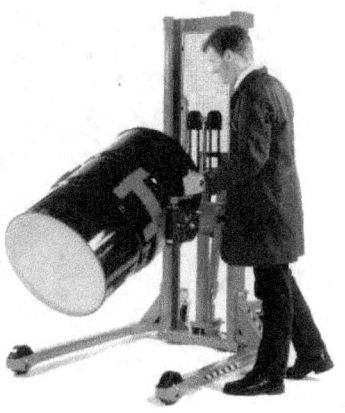

A drum lifter/rotator can lay the drum on its side. Add a spigot to the drum to empty its contents.

Some vacuum lifters have two handles and work best for lifts performed below mid-chest height within the power zone.

Vacuum lifters can handle sacks and bags that are hard to grip by hand.

Vacuum lifters make the handling of large or heavy containers easier.

Use a carousel.

Vertical carousels rotate and present items on shelves or roll out drawers within the worker's power zone.

Horizontal carousels rotate and bring items to the worker, eliminating walking and carrying loads.

Use a tilter.

Industrial tilters can improve access to large containers and make handling of materials easier. They can tilt up to 110⁰, but angles to 45⁰ are most common.

Some industrial tilters can also elevate so that containers or materials being handled are within the worker's power zone.

Resources

Appendix A Administrative Improvements

Administrative improvements include changing work practices or the way work is organized. Administrative improvements require continual monitoring by management and employee feedback to make sure the improvements are effective.

Provide variety in jobs

There are a couple of ways to increase variety in jobs. *Job rotation* means rotating employees through different jobs. *Job enlargement* means increasing the variety by combining two or more jobs or adding tasks to a particular job. To be effective, both improvements rely on changing jobs and tasks so that they differ in the:

- Muscles or body parts used
- Working postures
- Amount of repetition
- Pace of work
- Amount of physical exertion required
- Visual and mental demands
- Environmental conditions

Adjust work schedules and work pace

New workers who are not used to the physical demands of the job or those returning from long absences should be gradually introduced to a normal work pace and workload like an athlete in spring training.

Provide recovery time

Recovery periods (i.e., muscle relaxation periods) can help prevent fatigue and injury to muscles. Several short breaks can reduce the frequency and duration of physically demanding activities. Ask employees for their ideas for the best rotation or break schedules to reduce the physical demands of their jobs. Their suggestions can help you integrate the physical demands of jobs with the environmental and organizational demands of the workplace.

Modify work practices

Pay close attention to how the work is being performed. Employees should be encouraged to be comfortable, change positions, and stretch during work periods. The human body is stronger, more efficient, and less prone to injury when work is performed in *midrange* postures and within the *power zone*.

Midrange postures mean postures in which the joints of the neck, back, legs, arms, and wrists are not bent in extreme positions. The *power zone* is above the knees, below the shoulders, and close to the body. The principle of the *power zone* is that in this area workers have the greatest power to perform heavier work tasks with less bending, stooping, or reaching.

Appendix B Assessment Tools

NIOSH Manual Material Handling (MMH) Checklist
http://www.cdc.gov/niosh/docs/97-117/eptbtr5f.html

This checklist is not designed to be a comprehensive risk assessment technique but rather as a tool to quickly identify potential problem jobs. Additional risk factors may exist that are not accounted for in this checklist. It is common practice to follow up checklist observations with more precise techniques to confirm problem risk factors.

"No" responses indicate potential problem areas that should be investigated further.

1.	Are the weights of loads to be lifted judged acceptable by the workforce?	yes	no
2.	Are materials moved over minimum distances?	yes	no
3.	Is the distance between the object load and the body minimized?	yes	no
4.	Are walking surfaces level?	yes	no
	wide enough?	yes	no
	clean and dry?	yes	no
5.	Are objects easy to grasp?	yes	no
	stable?	yes	no
	able to be held without slipping?	yes	no
6.	Are there handholds on these objects?	yes	no
7.	When required, do gloves fit properly?	yes	no
8.	Is the proper footwear worn?	yes	no
9.	Is there enough room to maneuver?	yes	no
10.	Are mechanical aids used whenever possible?	yes	no
11.	Are working surfaces adjustable to the best handling heights?	yes	no
12.	Does material handling avoid:	yes	no
	movements below knuckle height and above shoulder height?	yes	no
	static muscle loading?	yes	no
	sudden movements during handling?	yes	no
	twisting at the waist?	yes	no
	extended reaching?	yes	no
13.	Is help available for heavy or awkward lifts?	yes	no
14.	Are high rates of repetition avoided by job rotation?	yes	no
	self-pacing?	yes	no
	sufficient pauses?	yes	no
15.	Are pushing or pulling forces reduced or eliminated?	yes	no
16.	Does the employee have an unobstructed view of handling the task?	yes	no
17.	Is there a preventive maintenance program for equipment?	yes	no
18.	Are workers trained in correct handling and lifting procedures?	yes	no

Hazard Evaluation Checklist for Lifting, Carrying, Pushing, or Pulling

This checklist is not designed to be a comprehensive risk assessment technique but rather as a tool to quickly identify potential problem jobs. Additional risk factors may exist that are not accounted for in this checklist. It is common practice to follow up checklist observations with more precise techniques to confirm problem risk factors.

"Yes" responses are indicative of conditions that pose a risk of developing low back pain. The larger the percentage of "Yes" responses that are noted, the greater the possible risk.

Risk Factors	YES	NO
1. General		
1.1 Does the load handled exceed 50 lb.?		
1.2 Is the object difficult to bring close to the body because of its size, bulk, or shape?		
1.3 Is the load hard to handle because it lacks handles or cutouts for handles, or does it have slippery surfaces or sharp edges?		
1.4 Is the footing unsafe? For example, are the floors slippery, inclined, or uneven?		
1.5 Does the task require fast movement, such as throwing, swinging, or rapid walking?		
1.6 Does the task require stressful body postures, such as stooping to the floor, twisting, reaching overhead, or excessive lateral bending?		
1.7 Is most of the load handled by only one hand, arm, or shoulder?		
1.8 Does the task require working in extreme temperatures, with noise, vibration, poor lighting, or airborne contaminants?		
1.9 Does the task require working in a confined area?		
2. Specific		
2.1 Does lifting frequency exceed 5 lifts per minute?		
2.2 Does the vertical lifting distance exceed 3 feet?		
2.3 Do carries last longer than 1 minute?		
2.4 Do tasks that require large sustained pushing or pulling forces exceed 30 seconds duration?		
2.5 Do extended reach static holding tasks exceed 1 minute?		

Source: T. R. Waters, "Manual Materials Handling", in: *Physical and Biological Hazards of the Workplace* (Second edition). Edited by P. Wald and G. Stave. New York: John Wiley and Sons, 2002.

Ergonomics Awareness Worksheet

The purpose of the worksheet is to increase basic awareness of potential problems associated with jobs and tasks. This awareness can help provide clues on how to make effective improvements.

Job Title: _____ Job Location: _____

Name of Employee: _____

Name of Observer: _____ Date: _____

Risk Factors	Other Clues	Reasons for Problems
Task 1:		
Task 2:		

Risk Factors	Other Clues	Reasons for Problems
Task 3:		
Task 4:		
Task 5:		

Adapted from *Easy Ergonomics: A Practical Approach for Improving the Workplace.* Sacramento: California Department of Industrial Relations, Cal/OSHA Consultation Service, Research and Education Unit, 1999.

Ergonomics Checklist — Material Handling

The checklist presented below is from the book *Kodak's Ergonomic Design for People at Work* (adapted from material developed by the Chemical Manufacturers Association). It helps users to identify any job risk factors that may be present in the job. This checklist is applicable to jobs requiring the routine handling of objects of 10 pounds or more.

Job/Task: _____ Dept: _____ Date: _____ Analyst: _____

Before _____ After (Controls Implemented) _____

Directions: Review each condition for the job/task of interest and for each condition that frequently occurs, place an X in the "Concern" column as appropriate. Add comments as appropriate.

Condition	X if a Concern	Comments
REPETITION		
High-speed process line or work presentation rates		
Similar motions every few seconds		
Observed signs of fatigue		
WORKSTATION DESIGN		
Work surface too high or low		
Location of materials promotes reaching		
Angle/orientation of containers promotes non-neutral positions		
Spacing between adjacent transfer surfaces promotes twisting		
Obstructions prevent direct access to load/unload points		
Obstacles on floor prevent a clear path of travel		
Floor surfaces are uneven, slippery, or sloping		
Hoists or other power lifting devices are needed but not available		

Condition	X if a Concern	Comments
LIFTING AND LOWERING		
Heavy objects need to be handled		
Handling bulky or difficult-to-grasp objects		
Handling above the shoulders or below the knees		
Lifting to the side or unbalanced lifting		
Placing objects accurately/precisely		
Sudden, jerky movements during handling		
One-handed lifting		
Long-duration exertions (static work)		
PUSHING/PULLING/CARRYING		
Forceful pushing/pulling of carts or equipment required		
Brakes for stopping hand carts/handling aids are needed but not available		
Carts or equipment design promotes non-neutral postures		
Long-distance carrying (carts not available)		
CONTAINERS/MATERIALS		
Lack adequate handles or gripping surfaces		
Are unbalanced, unstable, or contents shift		
Obstructs leg movement when being carried		
OTHER		
Inappropriate work techniques used		
Buildup of process material /product increases worker effort		
Personal protective equipment needed but not available/used		
TOTAL SCORE (Optional)		*To score, add up the total number of Xs identified.*

Appendix C Analysis Methods

The following methods are comprehensive tools designed to provide a detailed analysis of various types of manual material handling tasks. They can be used to evaluate lifting, lowering, pushing, pulling, carrying, and other activities.

NIOSH Lifting Equation

The NIOSH Lifting Equation is a tool used to evaluate manual lifting tasks. This equation allows the user to insert the exact conditions of the lift (e.g., height, distance lifted, weight, position of weight relative to body, etc.). This equation accounts for asymmetrical lifts and objects that are difficult to grasp.
http://www.cdc.gov/niosh/94-110.html

ACGIH Threshold Limit Values (TLVs) for Lifting

The American Conference of Governmental Industrial Hygienists (ACGIH) recommends guidelines for safe lifting. The Threshold Limit Values (TLVs) for lifting recommend upper and lower limits based upon frequency, duration, and other risk factors associated with lifting.
The following ACGIH Publications may be helpful:
    TLVs and BEIs (#0106)
    Lifting: TLV Physical Agents (7th Edition) Documentation (#7DOC-734)
To purchase publications, go to www.acgih.org/store or call (513) 742-2020.

University of Michigan 3D Static Strength Prediction Program

3D Static Strength Prediction Program software predicts static strength requirements for tasks such as lifts, presses, pushes, and pulls. The program provides an approximate job simulation that includes posture data, force parameters, and male/female anthropometry. The results include the percentage of men and women who have the strength to perform the described job, spinal compression forces, and data comparisons to NIOSH guidelines. The user can analyze torso twists and bends and make complex hand force entries. Analysis is aided by an automatic posture generation feature and three-dimensional human graphic illustrations.
http://www.engin.umich.edu/dept/ioe/3DSSPP/

Ohio State Lumbar Motion Monitor

Traditionally, most workplace ergonomic assessments have focused on joint loading in static postures. However, epidemiologic studies have shown that three-dimensional dynamic motion is associated with an increased risk of occupational injury and illness. The Biodynamics Lab has developed a unique research program that focuses on the study of occupational joint loading under realistic dynamic motion conditions. The program's goal is to obtain a better understanding of how much exposure to realistic risk factors is too much.

http://biodynamics.osu.edu/research.html

Snook's Psychophysical Tables

These tables are based on psychophysical data and provide the maximum acceptable weights and forces for various common tasks including lifting and lowering weights, pulling and pushing forces, and carrying objects. Values are given for different lift heights, number of lifts per minute, and percentiles of male and female populations capable of the task.

S. H. Snook, and V. M. Ciriello. "The Design of Manual Handling Tasks: Revised Tables of Maximum Acceptable Weights and Forces." *Ergonomics* 34(9): 1197–1213 (1991).

http://libertymmhtables.libertymutual.com/CM_LMTablesWeb/taskSelection.do?action=initTaskSelection

NIOSH Publications on Ergonomics and Musculoskeletal Disorders (MSDs)

NIOSH offers many types of publications including:
General ergonomics manuals
Industry or operation-specific manuals
Ergonomics texts

http://www.cdc.gov/niosh/topics/ergonomics/

Appendix D Improvement Evaluation "Tool"

As you evaluate possible improvement options, keep in mind the requirements that are most important in your particular workplace. Then, ask the following general questions for each improvement option under consideration:

Will this improvement:

- Reduce or eliminate most or all of the identified risk factors?
- Add any new risk factors that have not been previously identified?
- Be affordable for our organization (e.g., is there a simpler, less expensive alternative that could be equally effective)?
- Affect productivity or efficiency?
- Affect product or service quality?
- Provide a temporary or permanent "fix"?
- Be accepted by employees?
- Affect employee morale?
- Be able to be fully implemented (including training) in a reasonable amount of time?
- Affect the rate of pay or any collective bargaining agreements?

If you are thinking about new equipment for handling material, additional questions need to be answered. An evaluation will help to ensure that you choose the most appropriate piece of equipment to improve the "fit" between the task and the worker. For each improvement option under consideration, ask yourself if this particular piece of equipment will:

- Reach far enough to cover the work area?
- Handle the weight and shape of the product?
- Re-orient the load as needed for production (e.g., to empty or pour contents)?
- Be easy to load or unload?
- Require much force or energy to push it, steer it around corners, or stop it at the destination?
- Be heavy or large?
- Handle the load in a safe and controlled manner? Is the load held securely and is it well balanced? Will cables or chains allow too much movement compared with rigid links?
- Allow an adequate field of view for the operator?
- Slow workers down too much to meet production requirements?
- Interface with existing equipment and structures? Will weight-bearing columns, shelving, or other structures block the movement of the equipment?
- Need an additional power supply beyond what is currently in place?

Appendix E Organizations

The following organizations may provide additional information on material handling equipment and work practices.

American National Standards Institute (ANSI)
ANSI coordinates the U.S. voluntary consensus standards system, approves American National Standards, and is the sole U.S. representative and dues-paying member of the International Organization for Standardization and the IEC.
www.ansi.org

American Production and Inventory Control Society (APICS)
APICS — The Educational Society for Resource Management is a not-for-profit international educational organization that offers education and professional certification programs.
www.apics.org

American Society of Mechanical Engineers (ASME)
ASME membership includes opportunities to share new concepts, spearhead solutions, and advance the science and practice of mechanical engineering through the programs of its 36 technical divisions and four institutes. ASME International is a nonprofit educational and technical organization serving a worldwide membership of 125,000.
www.asme.org

Association of Professional Material Handling Consultants (APMHC)
APMHC is a professional society composed of individual consultants in the material-handling field.
www.mhia.org/PS/PS_APMHC_WhatIsAPMHC.cfm

The Automated Material Handling Systems Association
For over 27 years, the Automated Materials Handling Systems Association (formerly Automated Storage Retrieval Systems/Automatic Guided Vehicle Systems Users' Association) has promoted the sharing of knowledge and experience among its members, both users and vendors, to provide proven solutions to common warehousing/automation problems.
www.amhsa.co.uk

College-Industry Council on Materials Handling Education (CICMHE)
The council provides information, teaching materials, and various events in support of education and research on material handling.
www.mhia.org/et/ET_MHI_CICMHE_Home.cfm

Conveyor Equipment Manufacturers Association (CEMA)
CEMA's purpose is to promote voluntary standardization of conveyor design, manufacture, and application.
www.cemanet.org

Council of Supply Chain Management Professionals (CSCMP)

Council of Supply Chain Management Professionals seeks to enhance the development of the logistics profession by providing information and educational opportunities.
www.cscmp.org

Darcor and Ergoweb ® Ergonomic White Paper

The Ergonomics of Manual Material Handling - Pushing and Pulling Tasks
www.darcor.com/library_wp.htm

Fédération Européenne de la Manutention (FEM)

FEM is the European manufacturers association of materials handling and lifting and storage equipment. It represents the technical, economic, and political interests of the industry. FEM serves technical progress and improves safety at work through the establishment of guidelines and business codes.
www.fem-eur.com

Industrial Truck Association (ITA)

ITA's site includes directory of members' products by truck class, information on vendor-sponsored operator training programs, data on standards for trucks and parts, events of the lift-truck industry, annual statistics on U.S. shipments of industrial trucks, and more.
www.indtrk.org

Institute of Industrial Engineers (IIE)

The IIE is a professional society dedicated to advancing the technical and managerial excellence of those concerned with improving the productivity of integrated systems of people, materials, information, equipment, and energy. The IIE serves the professional needs of industrial engineers and all individuals involved with improving quality and productivity.
www.iienet.org

International Warehouse Logistics Association (IWLA)

The IWLA is the unified voice of the global logistics outsourcing industry, representing third-party warehousing, transportation, and logistics service providers.
www.iwla.com

Material Handling Equipment Distributors Association (MHEDA)

The Material Handling Equipment Distributors Association (MHEDA) is the only trade association dedicated solely to improving the proficiency of the independent material-handling equipment distributor.
www.mheda.org

Material Handling Industry of America (MHIA)

The MHIA is the nonprofit umbrella organization overseeing its two membership divisions: The Material Handling Institute (MHI) and the Material Handling Industry of America (MHIA). This vendor association's site includes a directory of MHIA members and its products as well as information on available literature.

The Material Handling Institute is the educational wing of the MHIA.
www.mhia.org

The following are product sections or councils within the MHIA:

Automated Storage/Retrieval Systems (AS/RS)

www.mhia.org/ASRS

Automatic Guided Vehicle Systems (AGVS)

www.mhia.org/AGVS

Conveyor Product Section (CPS)

www.mhia.org/CPS

Crane Manufacturers Association of America, Inc. (CMAA)

www.mhia.org/CMAA

Ergonomic Assist Systems and Equpment (EASE)

www.mhia.org/EASE

Hoist Manufacturers Institute (HMI)

www.mhia.org/HMI

Institute of Caster Manufacturers (ICWM)

www.mhia.org/ICWM

Integrated Systems & Controls Council (ICS)

www.mhia.org/ICS

Lift Manufacturers Product Section (LMPS)

www.mhia.org/LMPS

Loading Dock Equipment Manufacturers (LODEM)

www.mhia.org/LODEM

Monorail Manufacturers Association, Inc. (MMA)

www.mhia.org/MMA

Order Fulfillment Council (OFC)

www.mhia.org/OFC

Reusable Plastic Container and Pallet Association (RPCPA)

www.mhia.org/RPCPA

Storage Equipment Manufacturers Association (SMA)

www.mhia.org/SMA

Materials Handling & Management Society (MHMS)
The MHMS is an individual membership organization for the materials-handling
practitioner and the materials-handling community.
www.mhia.org/PS/PS_MHMS_Home.cfm

National Association of Manufacturers (NAM)
The NAM is the nation's largest industrial trade association, representing small and
large manufacturers in every industrial sector and in all 50 states.
www.nam.org

National Wooden Pallet & Container Association (NWPCA)

The NWPCA is dedicated to the success of its members by helping them create cost-effective, environmentally responsible solutions to meet their customers' changing unit load handling needs.

www.nwpca.com

Packaging Machinery Manufacturing Institute (PMMI)

The PMMI is a resource for packaging. PMMI's mission states that it is committed to improving, leading, and unifying all segments of the packaging industry worldwide.

www.pmmi.org

Robotics Industries Association (RIA)

The RIA is North America's only trade association focused exclusively on robotics. More than 250 member companies represent leading robot manufacturers, system integrators, end users, and researchers.

www.robotics.org

Society of Manufacturing Engineers (SME)

The Society of Manufacturing Engineers is a nonprofit, professional society dedicated to the advancement of scientific knowledge in the field of manufacturing engineering. SME is a professional society serving the manufacturing industries. SME has some 60,000 members in 70 countries and supports a network of hundreds of chapters worldwide.

www.sme.org

Supply-Chain Council (SCC)

The Supply-Chain Council's membership is primarily practitioners representing a broad cross-section of industries, including manufacturers, services, distributors, and retailers.

www.supply-chain.org

University of California Agricultural Ergonomics Research Center, UC Davis

This center's mission is to understand and apply ergonomic approaches to the development and evaluation of equipment designs and work practices that prevent musculoskeletal disorders in agricultural work.

The "pot lifter" was developed to lift and carry pots and other cylindrical containers. For detailed information on this device, go to http://ag-ergo.ucdavis.edu
Click on:

- Help for Industry
- Other resources for industry
- Tip Sheet 001:Nursery Lifting Tool (English and Spanish)

Warehousing Education and Research Council (WERC)

The Warehousing Education and Research Council (WERC) is the professional association for those in warehousing and distribution. WERC is a not-for-profit organization with more than 4,000 individual members.

www.werc.org

Acknowledgments

Writers and Editors

Zin Cheung, MS, CIE - Cal/OSHA Consultation Service - Sacramento, CA
Mario Feletto, MS, MPH - Cal/OSHA Consultation Service - Sacramento, CA
Jim Galante - EASE Council - Charlotte, NC
Tom Waters, PhD, CPE - NIOSH - Cincinnati, OH

Page Layout and Design

Jitan Patel - Cal/OSHA Consultation Service - Sacramento, CA

Photographers and Image Editors

Zin Cheung, MS, CIE - Cal/OSHA Consultation Service - Sacramento, CA
Rick Hight - Cal/OSHA Consultation Service - Sacramento, CA
Ken Jackson - Link One LLC - Sacramento, CA
Jitan Patel - Cal/OSHA Consultation Service - Sacramento, CA
Fran Wagner, MS, CIE - Link One LLC - Sacramento, CA

Editor

Faye Ong - CDE Press, California Department of Education - Sacramento, CA

Ergonomics Consultants

Suzanne H. Rodgers, PhD - Consultant in Ergonomics - Rochester, NY
Fran Wagner, MS, CIE - Link One LLC - Sacramento, CA

Editorial and Technical Reviewers

Dave C. Bare, CIH - Cal/OSHA Consultation Service - Sacramento, CA
David Brodie, MS, CPE - Atlas Ergonomics - Grand Haven, MI
Paul R. Burnett - Santa Clara Valley Water District - San Jose, CA
Fadi Fathallah, PhD - University of California - Davis, CA
Sean Gallagher, PhD, CPE - NIOSH - Pittsburgh, PA
Daniel J. Habes, MSE, CPE - NIOSH - Cincinnati, OH
John Howard, MD, MPH, JD, LL.M - NIOSH - Washington, DC
Ira Janowitz, PT, CPE - University of California - Berkeley, CA
Brian Roberts, C.S.P., CIE - CNA Insurance - Chicago, IL
Kristy Schultz, MS, CIE - State Compensation Insurance Fund - Sacramento, CA
Steve Smith, CIH - Division of Occupational Safety & Health - Sacramento, CA
Len Welsh, MS, JD - Division of Occupational Safety & Health - Sacramento, CA

Contributors

We thank the following people and organizations for their support and assistance in the development of this publication:

Denny Albrecht - BMH Equipment, Inc. - Sacramento, CA
Jim Borman - Signode Western Operations - Pittsburg, CA
Delia Deas - Tropicana - City of Industry, CA
Linda Donavon - Eagle Group - Clayton, DE
Ken Fletcher - Blue Diamond Growers - Sacramento, CA
Herman Jett - Cal/OSHA Consultation Service - Santa Fe Springs, CA
Mike Kelly - Calgene - Davis, CA
Ken King - SPC Industrial - Holly, MI
Rory Manley - General Pool and Spa - Rancho Cordova, CA
Etta Mason - Southern California Edison - Westminster, CA
Brad McCroskey - Triple A Containers - Cerritos, CA
Edward D. Page - Office of State Publishing - Sacramento, CA
Iraj Pourmehraban - Cal/OSHA Consultation Service, VPP - Oakland, CA
Fred Sibley - Natural Stone - Sacramento, CA

We thank the following companies for contributing to the development of this publication:

Acco Material Handling Solutions - York, PA
Accu-Sort Systems, Inc. - Tefford, PA
Advance Lifts Inc. - St. Charles, IL
American Lifts - Greensburg, IN
Autoquip Corporation - Guthrie, OK
Best Diversified Products, Inc. - Jonesboro, AR
Bishamon Industries Corporation - Ontario, CA
Bushman Equipment, Inc. - Butler, WI
Coffing Hoists - Charlotte, NC
Columbus McKinnon Corporation - Amherst, NY
Dalfuku America - Salt Lake City, UT
Dalmec, Inc. - Bloomingdale, IL
DC Velocity Magazine -Barrington, IL
Demag Cranes & Components Corporation - Solon, OH
Dematic Corp. - Grand Rapids, MI
Diamond Phoenix Corporation - Lewiston, ME
ECOA Industrial Products, Inc. - Hialeah, FL
Excel Storage Products - East Stroudsburg, PA
FKI Logistex Inc. - Saint Louis, MO
Gorbel Inc. - Fishers, NY
HK Systems - Milwaukee, WI
Hytrol Conveyor Company, Inc. - Jonesboro, AR
Ingersoll-Rand Company - Annandale, NJ
Intellegrated, Inc. - Mason, OH
Interlake Material Handling, Inc. - Naperville, IL
Interroll Corporation - Wilmington, NC
J&L Wire Products, Inc. - St. Paul, MN
Kingway Material Handling - Acworth, GA
Konecranes America, Inc. - Houston, TX

Lockheed Martin - Owego, NY
Lodi Metal Tech, Inc. - Lodi, CA
Material Handling Management Magazine - Cleveland, OH
Mecalux USA, Inc. - Melrose Park, IL
MegaStar Systems - Marietta, OH
Modern Materials Handling Magazine - Waltham, MA
Nashville Wire Products Manufacturing Co, Inc. - Nashville, TN
Pentalift Equipment Corporation - Buffalo, NY
Pflow Industries - Milwaukee, WI
Positech Corporation - Laurens, IA
Prest Rack, Inc. - Brookings, SD
Remstar International, Inc. - Westbrook, ME
Ridg-U-Rak, Inc. - North East, PA
Rite-Hite Corporation - Milwaukee, WI
S.I.T. Indeva, Inc. - Charlotte, NC
Serco - Carrollton, TX
Southworth International Group, Inc. - Portland, ME
SpaceRak, Division of Tarpon - Marysville, MI
Spanco, Inc. - Morgantown, PA
Speedrack Products Group, Ltd. - Sparta, MI
Steel King Industries, Inc. - Stevens Point, WI
Torbeck Industries - Harrison, OH
Unarco Material Handling - Springfield, TN
Unex Manufacturing, Inc. - Jackson, NJ
Vertical Systems International, LLC - Walton, KY
West Bend Division of Bushman Equipment, Inc. - Butler, WI
Wildeck, Inc. - Waukesha, WI
Yale Lift-Tech - Muskegon, MI

Cal/OSHA Consultation Programs

Toll-free number: 1-800-963-9424   Internet: www.dir.ca.gov

On-site Assistance Program
Area Offices

Northern California
2424 Arden Way, Suite 410
Sacramento, CA 95825
(916) 263-0704

Central Valley
1901 North Gateway Blvd., Suite 102
Fresno, CA 93727
(559) 454-1295

San Francisco Bay Area
1515 Clay St., Suite 1103
Oakland, CA 94612
(510) 622-2891

San Bernardino/Orange
464 West 4th St., Suite 339
San Bernardino, CA 92401
(909) 383-4567

San Fernando Valley
6150 Van Nuys Blvd., Suite 307
Van Nuys, CA 91401
(818) 901-5754

Los Angeles
10350 Heritage Park Dr., Suite 201
Santa Fe Springs, CA 90670
(562) 944-9366

San Diego
7575 Metropolitan Dr., Suite 204
San Diego, CA 92108
(619) 767-2060

Your call will in no way trigger an inspection by Cal/OSHA Enforcement

---

○ **Voluntary Protection Program**
  Oakland, CA 94612
  (510) 622-1081

○ **Research and Education Unit**
  Sacramento, CA 95825
  (916) 574-2528

DHHS (NIOSH) Publication No. 2007-131   **REU April 2007**